WHAT'S THE BIG IDEA?

HUMAN RIGHTS

Tim Cooke

Cavendish
Square

New York

Published in 2018 by Cavendish Square Publishing, LLC
243 5th Avenue, Suite 136 New York, NY 10016

© 2018 Brown Bear Books Ltd

Website: cavendishsq.com

CPSIA compliance information: Batch #CS17CSQ.

All websites were available and accurate when this book went to press.

Library of Congress Cataloging-in-Publication Data

Names: Cooke, Tim.
Title: Human rights / Tim Cooke.
Description: New York : Cavendish Square, 2018. | Series: What's the big idea?: a history of the ideas that shape our world | Includes index.
Identifiers: ISBN 9781502628244 (library bound) | ISBN 9781502628251 (ebook)
Subjects: LCSH: Human rights--Juvenile literature.
Classification: LCC JC571.C66 2018 | DDC 323--dc23

For Brown Bear Books Ltd:
Managing Editor: Tim Cooke
Editorial Director: Lindsey Lowe
Designer: Supriya Sahai
Design Manager: Keith Davis
Children's Publisher: Anne O'Daly
Picture Manager: Sophie Mortimer

Manufactured in the United States of America

CONTENTS

INTRODUCTION

In the 2010s, many people across the world enjoy certain universal rights. But this was not true for much of history. Today, people in some countries still have few rights.

Rights protect the freedom of people to behave as they wish. They also defend people from unfair treatment by others, whether individuals or governments. Experts identify numerous different types of rights. Civil rights, for example, guarantee social equality and the freedom to take part in politics. Sexual rights guarantee everyone the right to make decisions about what happens to their own bodies.

Human rights are the rights people have simply because they are alive. Human rights include the right to live and the right not to be enslaved or unjustly imprisoned.

In the 200s BCE the Indian emperor Ashoka erected a series of columns. They were carved with words that granted his people certain rights in life. →

People broadly have the right to act as they wish—as long as their behavior is legal and does not negatively affect other people. Adults have the right to stay awake all night, for example, but not to play music all night that disturbs their neighbors.

The need to prevent **terrorist** attacks like those on New York City on September 11, 2001, raises questions about the balance between rights and security. ↑

A long history

The first attempts to define human rights took place in the ancient world. By the early Middle Ages, which began in around 500, individual rights had largely been replaced by **absolute monarchies**. Kings had great power over their subjects. From the 1100s, however, kings increasingly had to give up power to keep the support of their **nobles**. Philosophers came up with new definitions of individual rights, which helped inspire revolutions in America and France. In the 1800s and 1900s, voting rights were gradually extended to poorer males and to women. Later in the 1900s, rights were widely granted to ethnic and sexual minorities. However, human rights were far from guaranteed even in important countries such as China and Russia, and the principles of human rights were particularly at risk of being ignored during civil wars and other conflicts.

WHAT ARE HUMAN RIGHTS?

Human rights are difficult to define. The simplest definition is that they are rights that everyone has simply because they are human.

In this definition, a human is a living person, whether male or female, or young or old. Rights are qualities or freedoms to which people are entitled simply by existing. The idea of human rights suggests that everyone is entitled to the same rights, regardless of where they live. In this definition, human rights are universal. However, for much of history that was not the case.

UNIVERSAL

Human rights apply to everyone, regardless of their race, sex, age, or nationality. →

Defining universal rights

A list of universal human rights was compiled for the first time in 1948 by the United Nations, or the UN. The rights were listed in a document called the Universal Declaration of Human Rights. They included familiar ideas such as freedom of speech (the right to say what one thinks) and freedom of religion (the right to follow whatever faith one believes in). But the declaration also defined more rights, such as the freedom to choose one's own partner, to live where one wants, and to do the job one wants. It also said that everyone was entitled to live free from **prejudice** and abuse.

Inventing human rights

The idea of human rights is fairly new. In the past, any rights that existed were not seen as being universal. The American and French Revolutions of the late 1700s were based on the idea that all men are born equal.

TIMELINE

1942 President Franklin D. Roosevelt uses the phrase "United Nations" to describe an international political body.

1945 At the end of World War II (1939–1945), the UN is **inaugurated** in New York City with 51 members. Today it has 193 members.

1948 The UN Convention on Human Rights publishes the Universal Declaration of Human Rights, a summary of 30 universal rights.

However, when the revolutionaries set out to define human rights in the 1700s, they excluded many members of society, including women, slaves, and, in America, native peoples.

The Universal Declaration of Human Rights came into existence as a result of the global devastation caused by World War II (1939–1945). The conflict caused the death of millions of people and displaced millions more, who were left homeless, stateless, and starving. Global leaders decided to create a global organization with the political authority to prevent future wars by providing a place where international disputes could be resolved.

DECLARATION

The US Declaration of Independence was based on the idea that no government could remove a person's right to "life, liberty, and the pursuit of happiness."

US president Franklin D. Roosevelt came up with the name "United Nations" in 1942, during World War II, when representatives of 26 nations fighting the Axis powers (Germany, Italy, and Japan) pledged to create a universal body. The UN was inaugurated in New York City on October 24, 1945, six months after Roosevelt's death. At the time of its founding, it had 51 members. It now has 193 members. Each member state pays a contribution toward the running of the organization.

UNIVERSAL DECLARATION OF HUMAN RIGHTS

In 1948, the UN Universal Declaration of Human Rights listed these 30 rights to which everyone is entitled simply by being human.

1. Right to Equality
2. Freedom from Discrimination
3. Right to Life, Liberty, Personal Security
4. Freedom from Slavery
5. Freedom from Torture and Degrading Treatment
6. Right to Recognition as a Person before the Law
7. Right to Equality before the Law
8. Right to Remedy by Competent Tribunal
9. Freedom from Arbitrary Arrest and Exile
10. Right to Fair Public Hearing
11. Right to be Considered Innocent until Proven Guilty
12. Freedom from Interference with Privacy, Family, Home and Correspondence
13. Right to Free Movement in and out of the Country
14. Right to Asylum in other Countries from Persecution
15. Right to a Nationality and the Freedom to Change It
16. Right to Marriage and Family
17. Right to Own Property
18. Freedom of Belief and Religion
19. Freedom of Opinion and Information
20. Right of Peaceful Assembly and Association
21. Right to Participate in Government and in Free Elections
22. Right to Social Security
23. Right to Desirable Work and to Join Trade Unions
24. Right to Rest and Leisure
25. Right to Adequate Living Standard
26. Right to Education
27. Right to Participate in the Cultural Life of Community
28. Right to a Social Order that Articulates this Document
29. Community Duties Essential to Free and Full Development
30. Freedom from State or Personal Interference in the above Rights

The stated aims of the UN are to keep peace and to protect human rights, but its activity also extends into areas such as protecting the environment and providing **humanitarian** aid during crises such as wars or natural disasters.

Changing rights

One of the first tasks of the UN was to define the human rights it pledged to defend. This led to the writing of the Universal Declaration of Human Rights. Since 1948, however, there have been many challenges to the idea of human rights and to world peace. Human rights abuses continue to take place in many countries. There have also been many wars since the 1940s, which have created **refugees** whose rights cannot be guaranteed by any government. The rise of terrorism in the second half of the 1900s also raised the question of whether those who practice or support terrorism should be entitled to human rights. The same question applies to those who carry out violent crimes, such as murder. Do such people forfeit their entitlement to human rights?

POSTER

Eleanor Roosevelt, who led the UN Commission on Human Rights, reads a poster of the Universal Declaration. →

Since its creation, the UN has been based in the UN Building in Manhattan in New York City.

The power of the state

Modern technology allows peoples' movements to be monitored. In some countries, the state uses this technology and its powers of **surveillance** to control its population. Such states see the rights of individuals as being less important than the rights of the state. Despite such challenges, the decades since the drafting of the Universal Declaration of Human Rights have seen many countries extend or improve the rights of women, ethnic minorities, and gay and **transgender** people.

IN SUMMARY

■ People are entitled to human rights simply because they are human.

■ The American and French Revolutions both asserted the idea that everyone had rights.

■ The first declaration of universal human rights came in 1948.

11

RIGHTS IN THE ANCIENT WORLD

The first definition of human rights was written down in 539 BCE. In that year, the Persian emperor Cyrus the Great conquered the city of Babylon.

After Cyrus conquered Babylon, he surprised his defeated enemies by announcing a series of plans to transform life in the **city-state**. Cyrus ordered that all slaves were to be freed and that citizens were now free to chose their own religion. He also declared all races to be equal in Bablyon. Cyrus's orders were the first expression of human rights. He had them recorded in Akkadian **cuneiform**, the written language of the Persians, on a cylinder made from baked clay.

CYLINDER

The Cyrus Cylinder has been broken and repaired. It is quite small: 9 inches (23 cm) long and 4 inches (10 cm) wide.

The text on what is now called the Cyrus Cylinder represented the first known example of a ruler giving his people some freedom to choose how they lived. Before Cyrus, kings had been absolute monarchs whose people had to obey their rule. For the many people who were owned by other people as slaves, there were no human rights at all.

Cyrus's ideas proved highly influential. A century later, the ancient Greeks absorbed the idea of individual rights into their ideas about **democracy**. Later, the ancient Romans would base their own form of democracy on that of the Greeks. Roman democracy helped to shape the democracies that emerged in the 1700s and 1800s.

In 1971, the declarations on the Cyrus Cylinder were translated into the six official languages of the United Nations. Its provisions are echoed in the first four articles of the 1948 Universal Declaration of Human Rights, including the rights to life, equality, liberty, and freedom from slavery.

TIMELINE

539 BCE — Cyrus the Great of Persia defines the rights of his subjects in Babylon. They are recorded on a small clay cylinder.

300s BCE — Aristotle and other Greek philosophers begin to think about the existence of a "natural law." It defined what was morally right or wrong.

262 BCE — In India, the Mauryan emperor Ashoka converts to Buddhism. He begins to introduce rights for his subjects, and even for animals.

Early rights in India

In the Mauryan Empire in what are now India and Pakistan, Ashoka became emperor in about 265 BCE. Ashoka had his many brothers killed so they could not challenge his right to be king. He became known for his brutal treatment of his subjects. In 262 BCE, Ashoka fought and defeated his enemies at the Battle of Kalinga, in the modern-day state of Odisha in northeast India. About 100,000 men died in the battle. Shocked by the loss of life, Ashoka turned his back on violence and converted to Buddhism. The Buddhist faith had been founded in India in the 600s BCE. It emphasizes nonviolence, fairness, gentleness, and social equality. Ashoka became an enlightened and inspired ruler, who stopped fighting wars and mistreating his subjects. He ruled his empire in peace for the next 40 years.

ASHOKA

Ashoka goes into battle with his troops. Having come to power through violence, Ashoka became a Buddhist and began a period of **benevolent** rule.

→

In order to tell his subjects about new laws that promoted a just, **humane**, and spiritually enlightened society, Ashoka issued proclamations called edicts. The edicts were carved on rocks and pillars throughout Ashoka's kingdom. They were placed in important locations.

Cyrus was named "the Great" for building the Persian Achaemenid Empire. The empire stretched across the Middle East and into Central Asia.

Ashoka wanted everyone to know about his new laws, which in many ways echoed those of Cyrus the Great. Ashoka's laws forbade violence, for example, and granted prisoners who were sentenced to death the right to appeal their punishment.
He encouraged his subjects to treat other peoples equally, and also forbade the killing of animals and birds that could not be eaten. This was the first ever expression of rights for animals.

DEMOCRACY TIMELINE

A series of steps helped advance the idea that people have the right to govern themselves through democracy.

1776 North America
North Americans claim the right to govern themselves, rather than be subject to British rule.

1789 France
The French revolt against their rulers, overthrowing the monarchy and the nobility.

ca. 300 BCE Rome
Rome introduces government by elected representatives rather than by direct democracy.

507 BCE Athens
Cleisthenes introduces reforms to allow Athenians to vote on important decisions.

The classical world

In ancient Greece, philosophers developed some of Cyrus's ideas about rights. In the 300s BCE, Aristotle argued that people in a society all follow an unwritten **moral** code that allows them to live side by side in a tolerant way. He also argued that natural justice is different from legal justice. This argument was based on what is called natural law—a system of justice based on principles of what is "correct," which people decide by using their reason.

Natural law applies to everyone and is based on the idea that humans have natural rights. Although ancient Greek city-states based their systems of justice and democracy on the idea of natural law, rights were not universal. Women did not have the same rights as men, slaves had no rights, and Greeks considered themselves superior to all other peoples.

ACROPOLIS

Athenians met on this rocky hill above Athens to vote on important matters—but only a small part of the population was able to vote.

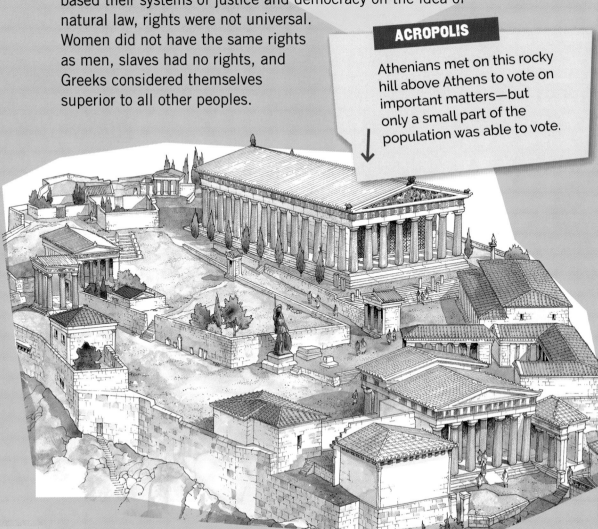

16

Only men over the age of 20 counted as citizens, which gave them the right to vote. Therefore, only between 10 and 15 percent of ancient Athenians could actually vote. Later, the Romans claimed to base their legal system on natural law, but rights were severely limited. In both ancient Greece and Rome, the majority of people were slaves with very few rights.

SENATE

Ancient Romans elected representatives to govern the Roman Empire on their behalf.

→

IN SUMMARY

■ Some of the earliest known attempts to define human rights came from ancient Persia and ancient India.

■ Persian ideas influenced the ancient Greeks, who came up with the idea of a "natural law." The Greeks passed their thinking on to the ancient Romans.

RIGHTS IN THE MIDDLE AGES

After the fall of the Roman Empire in 476 CE, Europe divided into weak kingdoms. Over some 500 years, strong rulers emerged. Supported by the nobility, they ruled as absolute monarchs.

By around 1000, kings had acquired great power over their subjects. They owned all the land in their kingdom, and distributed it among the nobles who supported them and fought on their behalf in times of war. In this **feudal system**, the vast majority of people were peasants who had few rights.

SIGNATURE

King John I of England was forced by his nobles to sign away some of his powers in return for their support in raising taxes. →

The situation began to change in the 1100s. In 1188, King Alfonso IX of Léon and Galicia, in Spain, caused riots when he imposed new taxes on his subjects. To restore order, he set up a **parliament** called the Cortes of León, which was made up of noblemen, clergymen, and representatives from towns. Under pressure from these advisors, Alfonso passed laws that gave the Cortes limited power over the king's actions. Some historians see this as the starting point of the introduction of democratic parliaments and political rights in Europe.

The Magna Carta

In 1215, King John I of England caused trouble when he tried to raise taxes to pay for wars he was fighting in France. The king's nobles rebelled against him. In May, they captured John's capital, London. The rebels forced the king to sign a charter acknowledging their rights to influence his decisions. The document was called Magna Carta, or "Great Charter."

TIMELINE

1188
King Alfonso IX of León and Galicia introduces a *cortes*, or parliament, that gives his subjects a say in how they are governed.

1215
King John I of England signs the Magna Carta, a document that limits the power of English kings and queens.

1200s
The philosopher Thomas Aquinas uses ancient Greek ideas as the basis for a new definition of natural law. It also incorporates Christian ideas.

The Magna Carta not only set out a number of new laws but also specified that those laws applied to everyone, including the king himself. Previously, monarchs had been thought of as being above the law. By signing Magna Carta, King John signed away the absolute authority of all future English kings and queens. He really had no choice but to sign because he needed the support of his nobles to raise taxes and fight wars. The charter made England subject to **constitutional law** rather than absolute rule. It also established for the first time that ordinary people had rights.

Rights for the citizen

The Magna Carta was written in Latin and contained 63 clauses, or points. These clauses offered equal legal protection to all free citizens by establishing the right to justice and a fair trial. It also introduced the law of **habeas corpus**. Anyone who was arrested had to appear in a court of law. The authorities had to show that there were good reasons for the person's arrest.

CORTES

Queen María de Molina presents her son, the future king Ferdinand IV of Castile and Léon, to the Cortes in 1295.

↓

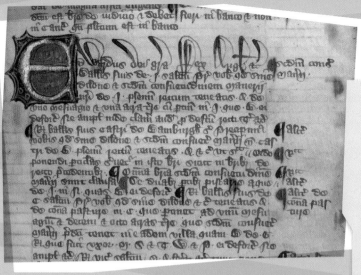

The law of habeas corpus was intended to protect people from being imprisoned on the personal decision of the king. Another clause protected the church from governmental interference and the government from the interference of the church. This is known as the separation of church and state. The Magna Carta also established the right for widows who owned property to choose to not remarry. This was a significant advance for women's rights at a time when most women were thought of as inferior to men.

FEUDAL SOCIETY

Medieval society was **hierarchical**. It is often imagined as a pyramid, with a few people at the top and the vast majority at the bottom.

ROYALTY
Monarchs
Princes   Princesses

NOBLES
Hereditary: Non-Hereditary:
Dukes and Barons   Knights

PEASANTS
Freemen   Serfs   Slaves

Many historians see the Magna Carta as a major turning point in the fight to establish human rights. Without it, parliamentary democracy may not have been established in England until after it appeared in the 1700s. The principles of the Magna Carta also influenced later documents such as the American Bill of Rights (1791) and the Universal Declaration of Human Rights (1948).

Thomas Aquinas

While the Magna Carta influenced political rights, the next step in the development of human rights came from the church. Thomas Aquinas (1225–1274) was a monk and philosopher from Italy who studied the ideas of ancient Greek philosophers such as Plato and Aristotle. Aquinas wanted to show how Greek ideas could be combined with Christian teaching, even though the Greeks had lived before Christianity existed. Aquinas wanted to show that humans followed natural law, not just the laws of God.

ARISTOTLE

Thomas Aquinas read the works of Aristotle (*right*), which had just become available in Europe in the 1200s having been preserved in the Islamic world. →

AQUINAS

Thomas Aquinas argued that people can prove the existence of God by observing the world and using their own reason. →

Aquinas discussed the concept of natural law using two Latin words: *rectum*, which means "morally right," and *jus*, meaning "what is just." Aquinas argued that natural law, *rectum*, applied to all things and people. Justice, *jus*, only applied in certain cases. Natural law aimed to establish what was "right," and also put forward the idea that all humans had rights.

Aquinas never developed his theories, but historians believe his ideas helped to pave the way for ideas about human rights. Those ideas started being circulated in the Age of Reason, or the Enlightenment, which began in the 1600s.

IN SUMMARY

■ Monarchs aquired absolute power in the early Middle Ages.

■ In the 1100s and 1200s, rulers surrendered some powers in return for the support of their nobles.

■ Thomas Aquinas developed Greek ideas of natural law.

23

THE RISE OF INDIVIDUAL RIGHTS

In the 1600s and 1700s, thinkers, writers, and scientists changed the way many people thought about human rights.

This was a period known as the Age of Reason, or the Englightenment. In the early 1600s, people in Great Britain, France, and elsewhere began to question the authority of both rulers and the Roman Catholic Church. Influential thinkers argued that humankind did not have to be subject to royal or religious laws.

EXECUTED

King Charles I was tried for ignoring the "liberties," or rights, of England. He was found guilty and beheaded in 1649. →

Instead, humans could improve life for everyone through **rational** thought. Thinkers could observe the world, identify problems, and develop solutions. The movement led to new scientific discoveries, new laws, and new ways to think about the world. It also led to disagreements between groups of people, causing wars and revolutions.

Revolution in England

In 1628, the English Parliament presented the **Petition** of Right to King Charles I. This statement of civil liberties tried to increase the rights of ordinary people at the expense of the king. It included the principles that only parliament could agree to impose taxes and that there could be no imprisonment without just cause. Relations between the king and Parliament broke down. The king dismissed Parliament in 1629 and did not call it again until 11 years later. Charles still refused to follow Parliament's wishes, however, and in 1642 war broke out between the king and the Parliament. Charles was captured and executed on January 30, 1649.

TIMELINE

1649 The English execute King Charles I during a civil war between the monarchy and Parliament over the king's power to rule.

1776 Great Britain's colonies in North America declare independence. The declaration defines "Life, Liberty, and the Pursuit of Happiness" as "unalienable rights."

1789 The French Revolution begins. The revolutionaries issue a Declaration of the Rights of Man and of the Citizen. It is based on Enlightenment ideas.

The English Civil War (1642–1651) ended in victory for Parliament. From 1649 until 1660, England was ruled as a commonwealth—a **republic** without a monarch—but in 1660 Charles's son was invited to take the throne as King Charles II.

The social contract

One influential thinker who questioned the idea of absolute monarchy after the English civil war was the English philosopher and physician John Locke. In his writings, Locke argued that humans had "natural rights" and that government was a positive force that controlled people for their own benefit. Locke saw this arrangement as a "social contract." The people allowed the government to enforce laws so long as the government made all decisions in the people's best interests. Locke also argued that people had the right to "life, liberty, and property." Both the social contract and the idea of natural rights would have a huge influence on Americans such as Thomas Jefferson, who were concerned about Britain's rule in its American **colonies**.

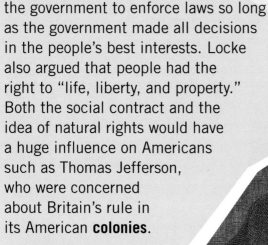

JOHN LOCKE

John Locke was one of the leading thinkers of the Enlightenment. His arguments about the social contract would influence world politics for centuries.

→

A colonial American reacts angrily to news of British taxes on American business.

←

KEY DOCUMENTS

The American Revolution

In 1775, colonial Americans rebelled against British attempts to impose new taxes, beginning the Revolutionary War (1775–1783). The Declaration of Independence, written by Thomas Jefferson and signed in 1776, explained why the Thirteen Colonies had decided to break away from Great Britain. He stressed individual rights and the right to revolt against unjust government.

In 1787, after the end of the war, the Founding Fathers signed the US **Constitution**. It is the oldest written national constitution still in use. It defined the system of government and law and the basic rights of every American citizen.

A series of key documents marked steady advances in the development of human rights.

1215 Magna Carta

1689 English Bill of Rights

1690 John Locke's *Second Treatise of Government*

1762 Jean-Jacques Rousseau's *The Social Contract*

1776 US Declaration of Independence

1787 Constitution of United States of America

1789 Declaration of the Rights of Man and of the Citizen (France)

1791 Bill of Rights (USA)

1791 Thomas Paine's *Rights of Man*

The rights enshrined in the US Constitution were clarified and expanded by the Bill of Rights of 1791, which set out the first ten amendments to the Constitution. It listed the freedoms from government interference to which a citizen was entitled.

Revolution in France

In Europe, the Revolutionary War and Jefferson's ideas about equality inspired the French Revolution (1789–1799). The revolution also reflected the influence of the Enlightenment and its use of reason to question accepted beliefs. In 1762, the French thinker Jean-Jacques Rousseau had written his own description of the social contract. He declared, "Man is born free and is everywhere in chains." When the French Revolution broke out in July 1789, the revolutionaries issued the Declaration of the Rights of Man and of the Citizen. This document set out the idea that "men are born and remain free and equal in rights."

CONSTITUTION

The US Constitution gave some rights to all persons in the United States, rather than just men. However, it only gave the right to vote to white males, and it did not recognize slaves as being fully human. →

The main target of the French Revolution was the extravagant rule of King Louis XVI and his queen, Marie Antoinette. They were executed in 1793, ending the French monarchy. The revolutionaries also killed many members of the nobility and destroyed the power of the Catholic Church. However, many changes were reversed when the monarchy was restored in the early 1800s.

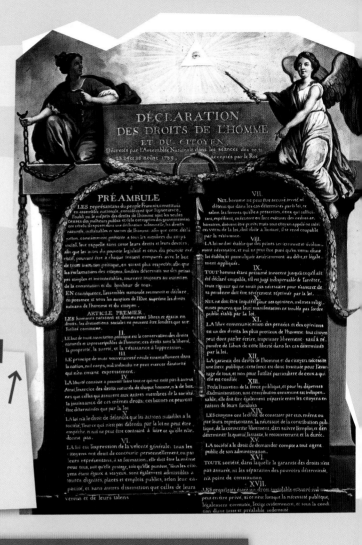

RIGHTS OF MAN

The French issued the Rights of Man and of the Citizen. It was based on the idea of natural law and saw human rights as being universal.

IN SUMMARY

■ During the Enlightenment, thinkers increasingly rejected the idea of absolute monarchy in favor of a "contract" between rulers and those they ruled.

■ Monarchs were overthrown in England and France. After the Revolutionary War, the United States was created without a monarchy.

FIGHTING FOR EQUALITY

By the 1700s, the fight to make all men equal was underway. In the early 2000s, many women and minority groups are still fighting for equal rights.

Most women in ancient cultures had no rights, although a few women became queens or the leaders of their people. Such women included Queen Cleopatra in Egypt in the OOs BCE and Boudicca, who led the Iceni tribe in the OOs CE as they fought the Roman invasion of Britain.

REBEL

Boudicca was a queen of the Celtic Iceni tribe who led an uprising against the Romans in Britain. Up to 80,000 Romans were killed before Boudicca died in around 60 CE.

In the early Islamic world some women played important roles as rulers and businesswomen. Later, Muslim women became subject to far more restrictions. In virtually all societies throughout history, women were denied education, were unable to own property, and were denied the right to vote. They were not allowed to have a bank account or to choose to divorce their husbands. Often societies considered women as being the property of their husband or of a male relative.

Votes for women

In the 1840s, women in the United States began to campaign for the right to vote, or suffrage. In Great Britain, women started to organize similar campaigns to gain suffrage from 1866. In fact, it was a British colony, New Zealand, that became the first country to grant women the vote in national elections in 1893.

TIMELINE

1863 During the Civil War, President Abraham Lincoln issues the Emancipation Proclamation.

1920 Women in the United States get the right to vote under the 19th Amendment. Some British women get the vote in 1918, but most have to wait until 1928.

1964 The Civil Rights Act in the United States forbids discrimination on the grounds of race, sex, religion, or national origin.

In both the United States and Britain, suffragists staged public protests to advance their cause. Despite the importance of the suffrage campaigns, however, it was the vital role played by women in World War I (1914–1918) that finally led to change. American women gained national suffrage in 1920, and in Britain women achieved equal voting rights with men in 1928 (although some women aged over 30 had been allowed to vote in 1918). Even today, a handful of countries still do not allow women to vote. Saudi Arabia only granted women limited suffrage in 2011.

African American equality

In the United States in the early 1800s, a divide developed between the northern states and the southern states about slavery. Over centuries, more than 10 million African people had been brought to the Americas as slaves against their will. Their descendants worked on cotton and tobacco plantations in the South, which depended on free slave labor. In the industrialized North, slavery was considered unacceptable. Eventually the argument led to the Civil War (1861–1865) and President Abraham Lincoln's Emancipation Proclamation of 1863, which freed the slaves.

PROTEST

Suffragists hold banners reading "Votes for Women" during a protest at Long Beach, New York, in 1912.

Despite achieving their freedom, African Americans continued to be treated like second-class citizens across much of the United States. They were unable to vote, had to attend **segregated** schools, eat in separate restaurants, and use separate bathrooms. They had to give up their seat on a public bus if a white person wanted it.

SOLDIERS

The 4th United States Colored Infantry was formed in Maryland in 1863. This group of men fought with the Union army during the Civil War.

CIVIL RIGHTS IN THE UNITED STATES

These laws and judicial decisions set out key advances in civil rights in the United States from the 1800s until today.

1863 Emancipation Proclamation

1870 15th Amendment grants the right to vote to all male citizens, regardless of their color or race

1920 19th Amendment gives women the vote

1924 Native Americans granted citizenship and right to vote

1960 Civil Rights Act reaffirms voting rights for all Americans

1964 Civil Rights Act outlaws discrimination on the basis of race, color, religion, sex, or nation of birth

2015 US Supreme Court approves same-sex marriage as legal in all 50 states

The Civil Rights Movement

It was another 100 years after the Emanciation Proclamation before African Americans properly gained their rights. The civil rights movement, led by Martin Luther King Jr., staged a series of nonviolent protests and marches to finally convince the government to pass the Civil Rights Act of 1964. The act outlawed **discrimination** on the basis of race, religion, national origin, or sex. The following year, the Voting Rights Act allowed African Americans in the South to register for the right to vote.

The United States was not the only country to discriminate against black people. In South Africa, black citizens were segregated from 1948 to 1991 in a system known as "apartheid," or "separateness." The system of government was based on the idea that black South Africans were inferior to the white South African minority. Black South Africans received the right to vote in 1994.

LGBTQ rights

The treatment of lesbian, gay, bisexual, transgender, and queer and questioning (LGBTQ) people has varied over centuries. In ancient Greece, for example, homosexuality was seen as the purest form of love. However, in modern times homosexuality has been considered illegal in most countries.

KING

Martin Luther King Jr. (center) was the main leader of the US civil rights movement.
→

PRIDE

Australians take part in an annual LGBTQ pride parade in Sydney. The parade celebrates LGBTQ rights.

The United States led the fight for gay rights. In 1969, riots at the Stonewall Inn in New York City led to the fight for gay rights becoming a national protest for equal rights. Since then, European countries have been some of the first countries to give gay people the same human rights as heterosexuals, such as the right to marry. In more recent times, many countries still consider homosexuality to be a crime. In all but five Muslim countries (Mali, Jordan, Indonesia, Turkey, and Albania) homosexuality continues to be illegal and punishable by arrest or even death.

IN SUMMARY

- ■ Women earned the right to vote largely as an acknowledgment of their contributions to the home front and military services in World War I.

- ■ Worldwide rights for minority groups lagged behind rights for the majority population. They were often only achieved through long protests.

HUMAN RIGHTS TODAY

It has been many years since the Universal Declaration of Human Rights. Do more people have more rights today?

Eleanor Roosevelt, the widow of US President Franklin D. Roosevelt, chaired the UN Commission on Human Rights that wrote the Universal Declaration of Human Rights. In 1948, she asked, "Where after all, do universal human rights begin? In small places, close to home—so close and so small that they cannot be seen on any maps of the world."

TERRORISM

The increasing frequency of terrorism raises questions about the extent people are willing to give up their rights in return for increased safety from attack. →

Eleanor Roosevelt was suggesting that human rights begin not on a national scale, but in everyday life— at school, in the workplace, and in the home. She argued that human rights must begin with people treating each other with respect and without discrimination.

On this level, it is difficult to judge how much the world has changed since 1948. In terms of legislation, there has been progress in many parts of the world in areas pertaining to rights for women, ethnic minorities, and gay people. However, countries such as Russia and China do not consider human rights a priority. There, the rights of the state take priority over those of the individual.

The threat of terrorism

One threat the UN did not foresee in 1948 was the rise of global terrorism in the late 1900s. National security forces now have increased powers to carry out secret monitoring of possible terrorist activity.

TIMELINE

2001 The US Patriot Act gives security agencies more rights to monitor citizens after the terrorist attacks of September 11, 2001.

2008 Upon becoming US president, Barack Obama promises to close the military prison at Guantanamo Bay. Over the next eight years, he fails to do so.

2015 The UN warns that the millions of refugees fleeing civil war in Syria are often not treated in other countries according to their rights as refugees.

This increased level of surveillance in society raises a moral dilemma about human rights. Is it justifiable to monitor innocent people in the hunt for possible terrorists? The Patriot Act was introduced in the United States after the terrorist attacks of September 11, 2001, on New York City and Washington, D.C. The act gave law enforcement the right to intercept emails, listen to phone calls, and even to monitor the books people take out of libraries. Many people have objected to the powers the act gave to the authorities to interfere in people's private lives.

Guantanamo Bay

Terrorism raises another question. Do terrorists who want to kill people, or have already killed many people, in the name of the cause in which they believe, have any human rights? If they are captured, should they be entitled to the same human rights as other people? Such issues have been asked about Guantanamo Bay, a US military prison on the island of Cuba. The camp is home to suspected terrorists, most of whom were captured in wars in Afghanistan and Iraq.

FIRST LADY

Eleanor Roosevelt defined human rights on a personal and local level.

←

PRISONERS

Most of the prisoners in Guantanamo Bay are being held without charge. If they do not stand trial, how can they challenge the authorities' belief that they are terrorists?

→

Prisoners at Guantanamo Bay can be detained there indefinitely without trial. This contradicts ideas about human rights that can be traced back to the Magna Carta. Critics of the prison demand its closure, but supporters argue that it is necessary to detain potential terrorists. President Barack Obama promised to close the camp when he became US president in 2008, but when he left office in 2017 it remained open.

WORST COUNTRIES FOR HUMAN RIGHTS

Amnesty International is a human rights organization. It rates all countries each year in terms of their respect for human rights. In 2016, these were the countries with the least respect for human rights, China being least respectful.

1. CHINA
2. EGYPT
3. HUNGARY
4. ISRAEL
5. GAMBIA
6. KENYA
7. PAKISTAN
8. RUSSIA
9. SAUDI ARABIA
10. SYRIA

There are also debates about the limits of human rights in daily life. Do people have a right to privacy when they use smartphones and computers to post private information on public social networks such as Facebook and Instagram? Should a person be stopped and searched in the street for looking suspicious? Is that an infringement of their human rights or a sensible policing policy?

Warfare and refugees

Some of the most serious challenges to human rights come during warfare. In the Rwanda **genocide** in 1994, members of the minority Tutsi people were murdered by the majority Hutu. In the Srebrenica Massacre of 1995, Bosnian Serbs murdered around 8,000 Bosnian Muslims during the wars in the former Yugoslavia.

In 2015, the UN warned that more people around the world had been forced to flee their homes by violence than at any time since World War II. The civil war in Syria in the Middle East forced millions of people to leave their country. In theory, such refugees should be protected by the terms of the 1951 UN Refugee convention.

SOCIAL MEDIA

If people put private information online, do they have a right to complain if the information becomes public or if it is used by businesses or governments?

←

The convention gives people the right to seek refuge from war and persecution. However, the convention was often ignored. Some European countries closed their borders to prevent refugees entering.

Many areas of the world remain where human rights are an aspiration rather than a reality. In 2016, organizations that monitor human rights said that human rights were still not recognized in around 20 of the world's 193 countries. There is still a lot of work to be done.

IN SUMMARY

■ Changes in society, from the growth of terrorism to the use of social media, created challenges to human rights in the early 2000s.

■ People displaced by warfare are vulnerable to losing their human rights. The same is true of people who live in states that put the rights of the state above those of the individual.

THE WORLD TODAY

Today, many countries around the world deny their citizens rights such as being able to oppose the governing political party.

North America

NORWAY In 2015, Norway topped the Democracy Index, followed by Iceland and Sweden.

Europe

GUANTANAMO BAY At the start of 2017, 45 prisoners were being held without trial at the US prison at Guantanamo Bay in Cuba.

45

Africa

THE DEATH PENALTY

Human rights campaigners oppose the death penalty because it goes against the right to life. In 2016, 140 countries had banned the death penalty. The countries that executed most people were (highest first): China, Iran, Pakistan, Saudi Arabia, and the United States.

South America

ARGENTINA In a "dirty war" from 1974 to 1983, the Argentine government killed left-wing opponents. Many were never found. There are thought to be 13,000 missing people, known as "the disappeared."

MEASURING HUMAN RIGHTS

Various organizations compile tables of human rights in various countries. They base their ranking on categories such as the level of democracy, the independence of the legal system, gender and sexual equality, and the treatment of non-citizens.

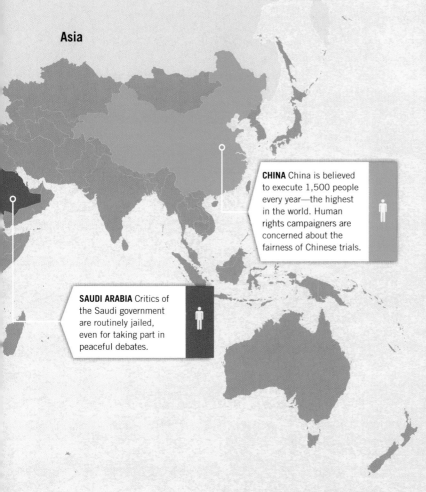

RUSSIA The government of Vladimir Putin shuts down opposing political parties and organizations that campaign for human rights.

Asia

CHINA China is believed to execute 1,500 people every year—the highest in the world. Human rights campaigners are concerned about the fairness of Chinese trials.

SAUDI ARABIA Critics of the Saudi government are routinely jailed, even for taking part in peaceful debates.

TIMELINE

539 BCE — Cyrus the Great of Persia defines the rights of his subjects in Babylon and has them recorded on a small clay cylinder.

300s BCE — Aristotle and other Greek philosophers begin to think about the idea of a "natural law" that everyone can recognize as being "right."

262 BCE — In India, the Mauryan emperor Ashoka converts to Buddhism and begins to introduce rights for his subjects—and even for animals.

1188 CE — King Alfonso IX of León and Galicia introduces a Cortes, or parliament, that gives his subjects a say in how they are governed.

1215 — King John I of England signs the Magna Carta, a document that limits the rule of English kings.

1200s — The philosopher Thomas Aquinas uses ancient Greek ideas as the basis for a new definition of the natural law, which incorporates Christian ideas.

1649 — The English execute King Charles I during a civil war between the monarchy and Parliament over the king's power to rule.

1762 — The French writer Jean-Jacques Rousseau writes, "Man is born free, but everywhere is in chains."

1776 — Great Britain's colonies in North America declare independence. The declaration defines "Life, Liberty, and the Pursuit of Happiness" as "unalienable rights."

1789 — The French Revolution begins. The revolutionaries issue the Declaration of the Rights of Man and of the Citizen. This document is based on Enlightenment ideas.

1863 — During the Civil War, President Abraham Lincoln issues the Emancipation Proclamation, declaring all slaves in the United States to be free.

1920	Women in the United States get the right to vote under the 19th Amendment. Some British women get the vote in 1918, but most have to wait until 1928.
1942	President Franklin D. Roosevelt uses the phrase "United Nations" to describe an international political body.
1945	At the end of World War II (1939–1945), the United Nations is inaugurated in New York City with 51 members. Today it has 193 members.
1948	The UN Convention on Human Rights publishes the Universal Declaration of Human Rights, a summary of 30 universal rights.
1951	The UN Convention on Refugees defines the rights of those who are forced to leave their homes because of war or persecution.
1964	The Civil Rights Act in the United States forbids discrimination on the grounds of race, sex, religion, or national origin.
1969	Riots at the Stonewall Inn in New York mark the emergence of a nationwide campaign for gay rights.
2001	The Netherlands introduces the first modern law allowing gay people the right to marry.
2001	The Patriot Act in the United States gives security agencies more rights to monitor citizens after the terrorist attacks of September 11 on New York City and Washington, D.C.
2008	Upon becoming US president, Barack Obama promises to close the military prison at Guantanamo Bay. Over the next eight years, he fails to do so.
2016	The UN warns that the millions of refugees fleeing civil war in Syria are often not treated in other countries according to their rights as refugees.

GLOSSARY

absolute monarchies Countries where a ruler has complete power over his or her people.

benevolent Kindly and well meaning.

city-state A political unit comprising a city and the region around it.

colonies Foreign territory ruled by a country.

constitution The basic principles by which a country is governed.

constitutional law Law based on the principles of a constitution.

cuneiform A form of writing created by pressing the end of a reed into soft clay.

democracy A system in which people are equal under the law and participate in government by electing representatives.

discrimination Unfair treatment of a group of people based on race, age, or sex.

feudal system A social organization in which all land is held in return for service to a king or a lord.

genocide The deliberate killing of a large group of people.

habeas corpus A law that requires someone who has been arrested to appear before a judge to check that the arrest is legal.

hierarchical Arranged in order of rank.

humane Showing compassion.

humanitarian Promoting human welfare.

inaugurated Introduced or opened.

moral Concerned with the nature of good and evil or right and wrong.

nobles The top rank of people in a society; aristocrats.

parliament A body that passes national laws.

persecution Ill-treatment based on someone's race, sex, or faith.

petition A written request for a change in law.

prejudice An opinion that is not based on evidence.

rational Based on logical thought.

refugees People who have been forced to leave their homes for safety.

republic A state governed by the people and their representatives, with an elected head of state.

segregated Kept apart on the grounds of race.

surveillance Close observation of people.

terrorist Describes acts of indiscriminate violence intended to spread fear.

transgender Describes someone who lives as a different gender from their birth sex.

FURTHER RESOURCES

Books

Braun, Eric. *Taking Action for Civil and Political Rights*. Who's Changing the World? Minneapolis: Lerner Publications, 2016.

Darraj, Susan Muaddi. *The Universal Declaration of Human Rights*. Milestones in Modern World History. New York: Chelsea House Publishers, 2010.

National Geographic. *Every Human Has Rights: A Photographic Declaration for Kids*. Washington, DC: National Geographic Children's Books, 2008.

Marisco, Katie. *Eleanor Roosevelt: First Lady and Human Rights Advocate*. Essential Lives. Edina, MN: Abdo Publishing Company, 2008.

Morlock, Theresa. *LGBTQ Human Rights Movement*. Civic Participation: Working for Civil Rights. New York: PowerKids Press, 2017.

Rodger, Ellen. *Human Rights Activist*. Get Involved. St. Catharines, ON: Crabtree Publishing Company, 2009.

Websites

www.amnestyusa.org/our-work
The home page of Amnesty International USA lists Amnesty's work as one of the main human rights organizations in the world.

www.ducksters.com/history/civil_rights/timeline_of_african-american_civil_rights.php
This Ducksters page provides a timeline of the fight for African-American civil rights in the United States.

www.historyforkids.net/womens-suffrage.html
History for Kids provides kids with the story of how women fought for suffrage.

hrlibrary.umn.edu/edumat/hreduseries/TB3/appendices/kidsversion.htm
This version of the Universal Declaration of Human Rights was written specifically for younger readers.

www.wisegeek.com/what-is-natural-law-theory.htm#didyouknowout
An explanation of the theory of natural law that began in ancient Greece.

http://www.youthforhumanrights.org/what-are-human-rights/universal-declaration-of-human-rights/articles-1-15.html
This website provides kids with a simplified version of the Universal Declaration of Human Rights.

Publisher's note to educators and parents: Our editors have carefully reviewed these websites to ensure that they are suitable for students. Many websites change frequently, however, and we cannot guarantee that a site's future contents will continue to meet our high standards of quality and educational value. Be advised that students should be closely supervised whenever they access the Internet.

INDEX